LONG-DISTANCE RELATIONSHIP INTIMACY HACK

HOW TO SURVIVE A LONG-DISTANCE RELATIONSHIP AND BUILD EMOTIONAL CONNECTION

By

Claire Robin

Copyright © Claire Robin – All rights reserved.

No part of this publication shall be reproduced, duplicated or transmitted in any way or by any means, digital or otherwise, including photocopying, scanning, uploading, recording and translating or by any information storage or retrieval system, without the written consent of the author.

Table of Contents

INTRODUCTION 4

HOW TO SHOW LOVE IN A LONG DISTANCE RELATIONSHIP. 6

USING THE POWER OF TECHNOLOGY 26

THINGS TO DO TOGETHER EVEN WHEN YOU'RE APART 31

RULES AND BOUNDARIES 45

SCHEDULING AND SETTING CONSISTENT COMMUNICATION... 51

HOW TO IMPROVE COMMUNICATION 55

RELATIONSHIP HACKS... 62

CONCLUSION 67

OTHER BOOKS BY THE SAME AUTHOR 70

CHAPTER ONE: LONG-DISTANCE RELATIONSHIP AND INTIMACY

LONG-DISTANCE RELATIONSHIP AND INTIMACY

Love is something so beautiful everyone wishes to experience, but it is not without challenges in every relationship. Relationships are always filled with ups and downs and in such times, the strength of both love and understanding is tested. Long distance relationships unlike relationships where the partners get to see each other frequently, is more demanding. It would take double efforts, understanding, trust and commitment to maintain them. However, there are many people in a long-distance relationship that managed to keep it going regardless of the hurdles. It just needs the effort of both parties and things will go smoothly.

If you're the only one striving to make things work, then chances are your relationship will come to an end eventually. Stay in a relationship where both parties are willing to fight for the blooming and thriving of the relationship. As the saying goes, it takes two to tango. There are times when relationships start as short distanced but due to certain life changes such as work transfers, new job offers or educational purposes, one partner is made to move away from another and serious adjustments will have to be made. Many relationships may even end due to this reason, but there are many equally that do thrive as a result of joint efforts. If you're looking for ways to revive and keep your long distance relationship blooming, then this book is for you.

CHAPTER TWO: HOW TO SHOW LOVE IN A LONG DISTANCE RELATIONSHIP

HOW TO SHOW LOVE IN A LONG DISTANCE RELATIONSHIP

Being separated from your partner by miles can prove very challenging and demanding. You will certainly have a thousand questions on how you are going to cope with the distance, absence and lack of proximity, especially if physical touch is of utmost importance to you. People interpret love differently, and what works for one may not necessarily work for the other. So taking the first step of finding out what works for you and your partner, will help you understand better how to show them love no matter the distance.

As Gary Chapman stated in his book **THE 5 LOVE LANGUAGES**, everyone has a language of love they respond to. It is very possible to have more than one love language, but there is always the primary language you prioritize over the rest, the one that makes you feel the most loved. The language your partner uses in relating to you is most likely their own love language, and the language you use in relating to your partner, is most likely yours as people tend to show love based on their own definition of love. In a case where your partner expresses his love for you by giving you gifts when your primary love language is quality time and attention, you may end up feeling he does not love you enough and this is why communication is crucial in every relationship. Deciding to go into a long distance relationship or continuing in your relationship when circumstances has forced it to become long distance means that both you and your partner have decided to take responsibilities and put in effort to make it work. So talking about how best you feel loved, should not be a challenge. Do not joke with the place of communication in your relationship, if you do not want to wake up to a partner that has gradually become a stranger to you, as communication is also a strong form of intimacy.

Here are some ways to show love to your partner in a long distance relationship:

1) **Keep constant communication:**
Yes, I am emphasizing on it again. The mistake of disregarding communication in a relationship has led to the end of many relationships, as this affects your relationship as a whole. It determines how weak or strong your relationship turns out to be. This becomes even more vital when your partner portray his/her love language through quality time. Experts will tell you not to choke up your partner with keeping tabs on them and demanding to know everything they do or make talking every day mandatory. This is also true, but sharing your experiences everyday with your

partner and reminding them that they're a crucial part of your life makes them feel loved, and strengthens your bond. There are various means that can be used for maintaining communication; texting randomly during the day and sending them funny or intriguing details of your day as you experience them, sending voice notes as you chat or using voice calls as this comes with its own special feel--video call is also a good means of closing the gap between you. It is advised to be friends with your partner as this is what will keep you both together in the long run. Even if you fall into the category that started off as strangers on the first date, take your time to become friends with your significant other. If efforts are put in jointly, there is no barrier that can stand in the way of your relationship.

2) **Do it the old fashioned way:**
Remember when handwritten letters were a thing for lovers? How they earnestly anticipated the date for the arrival of a new letter? When mobile phones were not so much in circulation? Well, what's stopping you from going the old fashioned way now? There are many people who appreciate handwritten letters and DIY cards than the random electronic letters and messages we have these days. Mostly because a handwritten letter takes extra effort, it passes the message to your partner that you will put in the time to do something different for them. So do it the old fashioned way, mail them a letter written on scented paper with stickers and carved out images displaying affection. They would spend time laughing at how cheesy it looks and how

heartwarming it feels to be thought about. Do not push this off because you feel you shouldn't spend so much energy on something that can easily be done electronically, the extra spice and variety they say is the color of life.

3) Stay involved in each other's lives:

This goes for every relationship be it long distance or not. It is crucial to be more intentional about this in a long distance relationship since the distance might make it easier to lose touch with your partner's affairs. Do not just take time in talking and sharing about your day, ask them about work, business, dreams, plans, the progress they're making and how they might need support, be it intellectually or emotionally. Your interest in their lives will go a long way in showing that you care, and count their affairs as yours too.

Many times, your partner might need some motivation to push on with a particular plan he is procrastinating or even kick start his big dreams. Stay involved, encourage him, check the progress of projects with him and draw out deadlines for every project together. You might not realize how effective this is in building your relationship, but in the long run you would be thankful you became involved in your partner's life. Becoming actively involved in your partner's life makes it easier for them to open up to you a great deal, and it also makes it easier for you to share in their joy and pain, wins or loses alike. It builds a unique sense of partnership, and team spirit. This is also important because you are now one of the most important persons in the life of your partner, and showing him you're interested in his life and affairs, tells him that you want all parts of him, and that place a huge importance on his growth and success.

4) The Social media perks:

This entails all the upsides of social media especially in keeping your relationship fun filled and interesting. There are various features you can use online to spice up your relationship and make your partner feel involved in your life all day long. Do not wait for special occasions to randomly post them on your status with a caption of how much you appreciate and adore them, tag them to your posts and mention them on funny posts and memes you know might interest them. Send funny pictures of things you come across on your chats randomly, hit them up with the weirdest thoughts or encounters you have and laugh over them together. Send them your funny snapchats, videos and pictures alike with you making goofy faces or looking all cute and do not fail to repost some of them you really like with endearing comments. Make your partner feel like a huge part of your life, and you would see how the huge issue of distance gradually becomes so little.

5) **Visit regularly:**

No matter the distance between you and your partner, make it a priority to always visit regularly. You can also seize this option to pay them surprise visits especially when they might have repeatedly complained to you about a recent challenge they're showing. Your unexpected appearance might just be the sunshine walking through their door. It is advised to make it a point to see each other at most, every three months. It is not ideal to stay away from each other for too long as physical touch as simple as holding of hands and hugging are also strong bond builders. The physical presence of your partner from time to time is very important and this is not a vacuum that virtual communication can fill. If it then happens that your partner's primary love language is physical touch, you would have to pay more attention to this as your relationship does not only exist for you, but for the other person too. But whether this is your love language or not, do not stay away from your partner for so long. Plan about it together, set out dates when one of you takes time off work or school to visit the other, take turns visiting, and pick surprise dates too for a visit.

6) Stay reassuring:

Women might have a deeper need to be constantly reassured than the men do, but the bottom line still remains that both gender crave reassurance. Making it a custom to constantly tell your partner that you love them, adore them, miss them, appreciate them, and can't wait to spend more time with them in person. Let the "I love you" flow freely in your relationship, as those simple three words carry a power hearts are yet to explain. Your partner might not lay demands on you or question you, but randomly remind them that they're the only ones for you and no one else can take their place. Reassurance does your partner a whole lot of good, and kicks away fear or doubt from your relationship. Nobody wants to be the desperate partner always asking and checking during tough situations if their partner is still in love with them, so your partner will likely not ask you questions of reassurance. It is left for you to always remind them of the special place they hold in your heart, and this goes beyond just saying. Let your actions be warm and reassuring too, not distant and cold.

7) **Maintain trust:**

You have to understand that putting your heart in the hands of another person and going far away is no trivial matter. Your partner made a choice to trust you against all odds the day he decided to commit to you, and it is very important that you do not take that trust for granted. Do your best to avoid places, people, or encounters that are capable of putting you in a compromising position. You do not want to give your partner reasons to begin doubting you, and you do not want to put your relationship at risk. No matter how head over heels you are about a person, no relationship thrives without love and trust working hand in hand. So love is not enough here, cherish the trust in your relationship and protect it fiercely. If you have friends that are constantly trying to push you into activities that will risk your relationship, then you have to take a step away from them. Unless in cases where they are not aware that you are now committed to a person, which should not be so. If your friends are well aware of your relationship and are still trying to push you into unreasonable activities, then they might just be the very bad influence you want to avoid for the sake of your relationship and more importantly, future. Maintaining trust here does not just lie in staying worthy of your partner's trust, it also involves trusting your partner completely. It is highly risky to be in a long distance relationship with someone you do not truly know or trust as you might just be investing years or tangible months of your life into nothing. But if you know this person well enough and have found them worthy of your trust, you should be able to keep it that way. Avoid unnecessary suspicions and poking, mistrust and the likes that will bring you heartaches and eventually hurt your relationship.

8) Stay faithful:

It is true that temptations will always come and of course, one is only human. But you will have to keep in mind that another human being, has placed their heart in your hands. If there are any issues in your relationship, any need that is not being met, any complaints, talk it out with your partner. Avoid seeking attention and intimacy from any third party as there are no excuses whatsoever for being unfaithful. If you fall into this trap, it is as good as saying you made the choice yourself. Your partner is going against all odds to trust you, and you do not want to make them regret their decision. People do not understand that breaking of trust through unfaithfulness hurts the person being betrayed beyond the drama that plays out when they find out. It can leave a long lasting scar, and affect their future relationships or their view on love and life generally. You do not want to be the one to cause such a damage to another human being.

9) Send Gifts:

They might be few or much as the case may be, but there are still a good number of people who find it hard to request for things from their partner, especially in the stage of dating. Taking the hint to send gifts and care packages on your own, will be a plus for you in the heart of your partner. Send gifts on special days of course, but do not always wait for those days to send a package to your beloved. Gifts on special days may be expected, but imagine your sweetheart receiving a parcel on a random sunny day at work, or task filled and strenuous evening after school. Imagine the smile it would put on their faces and the love that would fill their hearts. Gifts do not always have to be expensive or plush, but they should always convey how much you love your partner. Pay attention to your choice of gifts too, try as much as possible to send a gift that sparks up a memory you both have shared together or one of the memories you hope to share, in time to come. Attach notes to your gifts, spilling how much you adore and believe in your partner. Well, doesn't love make one a poet? Go on and spill those tiny poems your heart is weaving. A gift can also be an online transfer on a rough day, or a particular bill payment. But no matter what you do online, do not fail to also send a smiling package to your partner, from time to time.

10) **Carry out activities together:**

It is easy to set dates, go on picnics, see a movie together, in a short distance relationship. But when the reverse is the case, it can become difficult for couples who are not social media fans. However, it is never late to adapt to new methods to suit the changes in your life. There are lots of activities to carry out together with your partner notwithstanding the distance. Game apps now have the feature of playing with friends over a distance, Skype provides a good chance to video call and carry out activities virtually, you can also pick the same books to read, and talk about your views on the book. Share your playlist with your partner, share your favorite songs and create a playlist to keep tracks that you both love. Be intentional about it, and let your partner create his own copy of your together lists for song you both share a passion about. Pick a time to see a movie together, consider virtual dates and enjoy them like they were physical. Take your mind off the distance and focus on all you can do together from a distance. You would be thankful for the bond it creates and the tension it eliminates.

11) Love beyond your partner:

This should be within certain boundaries though, especially when your relationship is still at its early stage. Nonetheless, your love for your partner has to stretch beyond them to their families and loved ones. If your partner has a worry about their family and you happen to be close to them even though your partner is far away, step in and help if you can. Supporting them in such times will help relieve the stress on them and your relationship too as a man worried over his family is hardly any fun to you too. If your relationship has gone so far on solid grounds and you both have been introduced to families on the verge of being joined together, you might want to consider bonding with his family too, if they are accommodating. This bonding goes both ways for you and your partner. You cannot profess to love someone and not love the people they hold dear to their hearts too. Showing the same amount of care your partners will show to their families, is a very significant and effective way to show them how much you love them, and the people or things they love too.

12) Stay patient and understanding:

This is one of the important traits you will have to display, so if your patience level is very low, you had better started working on it. Long distance relationships will demand a high level of patience, understanding, and maturity too if I may add that to the list. Well, two intellectually and emotionally immature adults can hardly make a relationship work, so if you are in a relationship and a long-distance one at that, it is expected that you exude a high level of maturity and self-control. There are times when your partner might be caught up with work and not be able to meet up with together-times or usual phone calls and texting. This would not be easy on you as you depend on these things to close up the gap between you two. It is only natural to want to get edgy, and this is where understanding and patience comes in. Understand that it is not their fault, and things will not always be that way.

CHAPTER THREE: USING THE POWER OF TECHNOLOGY

USING THE POWER OF TECHNOLOGY

One added advantage modern day couples have, is that of technology and social media perks. As emphasized before, communication plays a vital role in every relationship especially in a long distance relationship. Distance is a factor that can put a strain on couples, and test their level of trust and patience. Without communication, it is almost impossible to maintain trust, a deep connection, or to even survive this test. Gone are those days when distance keeps you panting and uncertain. Technology has provided a way for partners to stay deeply connected over a thousand miles. Yes, your new job offer should not be an end to your relationship as long as your partner shares the same passion, and is willing to follow the steps of maintaining the bond of your relationship, no matter the distance. Technology exists to provide ease for mankind, and one of those benefits is communication within a long distance. This was not so in times of old as they had to depend on snail mails, expensive phone calls, and long awaited letters. We are given the chance now to send messages that get delivered in seconds, talk for long hours over the phone at cheap rates, and even see your partner regularly on video calls. Knowing this and using it to the full advantage of your long distance relationship, is knowing peace.

Inasmuch as texting and sending of voice messages should be maximized, they should not take the place of long and interactive phone calls. There is a special feeling that comes with talking to your partner and hearing them respond immediately or even laugh and giggle to your comments. There are people who prefer texting, and whether or not you are one of them, healthy phone calls are still advised. Do not also fail to pay attention to the needs of your partner and their own preferences. There is also the place of video calls, Skype, Facetiming for users of iPhones, and other means of seeing your partner from time to time. It feels different when you're able to see their faces and reactions during conversations and not just still pictures being sent to you. Video calls also help with reviewing books you've set out to read with your partner, keeping them involved in places you visit, and activities you partake in. This feature is also a plus because it can be used for virtual dates with your partner. Being intentional about enjoying your relationship and not stress so much about the distance gives you time to explore these features and maximize the place of technology.

There are also virtual games to play with your partner, as many game apps allow you compete with friends over a long distance. With features like this and more, you can enjoy your relationship over miles and find healthy ways to sustain your bond. New trends are making cyber-sex a thing and even though this might feel creative and fun to you and your partner, it is really not advised. In some countries, local laws are against cyber-sex and even if they're not, there are religious reasons why you should not partake in this. Sexting or other forms of cyber-sex can also set expectations that you might not be able to meet up to when you're finally with your partner. If you're looking to stay away from sex till after marriage, then you should not give your partner the impression that you would give him sex if it were not for the distance. Cybersex can also be frustrating as you stir yourself or even turn your partner on without any true satisfaction at the end, and this has more downsides than upsides. There is also the risk of your colleagues, friends or even employers stumbling on your conversations with your partner and even though this is less likely, you don't want to go through the risk of losing your privacy. Your partner on the other hand might not be as serious as you are with protecting their device, and his own copy of your conversations can be read. This does not only pose a risk of loss of privacy, but can also pose an issue at his place of work depending on who stumbles onto your sexts. There are many fun-filled ways to enjoy your relationship without having to cross healthy lines, so it is advised that you use them to the maximum. Technology has provided you with ease in communication and it gives you the power to keep your relationship flourishing, and communication with your partner consistent.

CHAPTER FOUR: THINGS TO DO TOGETHER EVEN WHEN YOU'RE APART

THINGS TO DO TOGETHER EVEN WHEN YOU'RE APART

Keeping a long distance relationship going can become more demanding than a short distance relationship because the number of times you would see your partner in a year is limited, so carrying out activities together will have to be intentional as your partner is not always physically present. There are hundreds of things to do together even over a really long distance, that would snatch the power from the thousand miles between you and your partner. Activities you carry out with your partner should not just be limited to texts, calls, or video chats. There are many other fun and intimate activities as well as productive ones to carry out, to strengthen your relationship.

1) **Read books together:** A saying goes "Your conversations are as good as the books you read" and it is very true. Be it from reading, listening or watching movies or other informative videos, you

can only give out as much knowledge as you take in. One of the advantages of a long distance relationship is that it gives you the chance to build a healthy relationship, while still having the space and time enough for your own personal growth. It is impossible to read hundred books and remain the same way. So what better way to grow than with the one you love? Starting a book club with your partner gives you the chance to share extra moments with them, while staying productive. You can decide to read some chapters together over a video chat, or just stick to reading separately and doing reviews together. Sharing excerpts from the books you read with each other can be exciting too or picking specific chapters to read together on same dates. However, you want to shuffle your book reading activities to make them more fun and exciting, feel free to go all the way.

2) Engage in quiz and intellectual activities: This might not work for some people as they might just want all fun and no stress, but setting up a quiz for your partner and they doing the same for you can be bucket full of fun too. There can be a prize for the person with the highest scores. Keep the rewards simple and fun filled, to maintain the excitement. If your partner's voice is not so cool for singing, you can demand your reward be a song from them and get the opportunity to share hearty laughter together, you can request for a bar of chocolate delivered to you or brought on the next visit, you can also turn it around and ask them to do a particular thing for themselves that they've pushed away for too long as their growth is yours too. Feel free to engage in logical arguments with your partner over video or voice calls. Share your views about the world or philosophies and let them disagree with you with their own views and beliefs. All these gives you a chance to know your differences and similarities alike, learn their own view of life, and understand how they think better. It is important to know that your partner was born and raised quite differently from you, is an independent human being with his own train of thoughts, and will not always share the same views as you. Accepting this and enjoying your differences instead of capitalizing on them, will be much to your advantage.

3) **Go on dates with your partner**: It is normal if your ideal date is one in which you hold hands across the table as you eat, share food and drink from the same glass or plate, hug tightly at the end of the day, or even interlock fingers. But if your relationship is long distance, it shouldn't stop you from enjoying beautiful dates with your partner, thanks again to technology. You can plan virtual dates with your partner, wear that lovely dress you would have picked if they were physically present, and pick a nice restaurant or bar. You can have your partner do the same on an agreed date

and time, and eat together over a video call. You would have to be prepared for this as the call will last all through the date. Set a stand for your phone that allows both hands to be free while you are still able to see your partner. Pick whatever it is you would have picked, talk and laugh together, eat, make a toast, and intentionally enjoy every bit of your date. This is not unrealistic, but still very enjoyable. It depends on what you've made up your mind to capitalize on, your relationship or the distance between.

4) **Watch movies together:** Again your idea of seeing a movie with your partner can be popcorn and cuddles, in a huge cinema or on the couch, with a huge bottle of coke shared together. But who says you can't have your movie dates or time with your partner over the distance. You can send lists of interesting movies you come across to your partner, and let them do same. Pick a time when you're both free and off work, pick a movie you'd like to see

together, and watch from both ends over a video call. You might not want to stay on the call all through the movie especially if it's very lengthy, but ensure to start it together over the video call, to check on each other midway, and towards the end. As you do so you can go all the way to share your views and critics about the movies as well as the intriguing and thrilling parts. If you pick a series, you might want to pick dates for seeing an episode at a time with your partner. Whichever works for you, understand that it's your relationship and up to you to keep it interesting.

5) **Share pictures and videos**: Nothing lights up your day more than the face of your sweetheart on your screen during a hard day at work or school. Normalize sending your partner pictures of yourself occasionally. You can send them pictures of your activities or you indulging in them, pictures of your lazy or crazy moments, weird stuff you encounter or funny

ones alike. Send pictures of you making goofy faces or sharing time with friends. Nothing keeps him happier than knowing that even when you're hanging out with friends so far away from him, you still have him in heart and want to share every moment with him. Make short video clips of yourself looking all cute and funny, or doing something nice and productive. Your partner will definitely have a good time viewing your pictures, laughing over funny videos and even repeating them. Know that you can also send interesting videos and pictures you stumble on online, and not just those of yourself. Whenever you come across pictures or videos that you know your partner might find funny or interesting, do well to save and share with them.

6) **Stay on the line**: This is how I'd like to put your calls and video chats with your partner. Looking for what to do with your partner over the distance, call and video chat with them. Nothing is more soothing than the voice of the one

you love, and laughing with someone sharing hearty moments with you while being able to see the spark in their eyes is something beautiful. Set out quality time to call your partner and share deep moments with them. This is an important part of keeping your connection going and even though you shouldn't literally stay online and on their necks at all time, make sure you're having enough voice time and face time with your partner. Keep it moderate, but from time to time do call your partner when you have a question about what to do or you're having a challenge fixing something. This is important as it makes them feel needed even over the long distance. They may never tell you, but they would always feel extra happy when they know they're the ones who come to mind when you need help with a tough situation.

7) **Play online games together**: This is another fun filled activity you can carry out with your partner irrespective of

distance. Game apps now have features that allow you to play with friends from your phone. You can even make this more exciting sometime by inviting your mutual friends to join in on the games if you want to. You will find this thrilling and fun filled. Pick a time when both you and your partner are free, and catch exciting moments together. If you're having issues with setting this up because you're not conversant with the way the apps work, you can ask for help from friends or directions from your partner.

8) **Prepare meals together**: Look for new recipes online and prepare meals together over video chats. This is another exciting activity especially if your partner does not know how to cook, and is interested in learning. The first awkward attempts will send you laughing for a long time, and of course healthy teases are okay. Try out new dishes together, prepare the same thing and share how they taste. Create your own recipes if you want to make it

more exciting, and find out how creative you and your partner can be. You can pick specific days in the week when you both have the time to prepare either breakfast or lunch together, and eat together too. Sharing the same meal with your partner over the long distance will bring you a sense of closeness and intimacy.

9) **Talk about your future together**: You do not want to put so much effort and emotions into a relationship that is not defined or heading anywhere. Most likely, you and your partner are dating to check your compatibility for marriage. If this is the case, then you should talk about how you picture your future together to be. This talk is not limited to how you want your marriage to be though, you should share where you see yourself in your career and other dreams you have in years to come. If your vision is to travel the world, now is the perfect time to tell your partner that this is how things are going to be. Give them a chance to

decide to love you notwithstanding the crazy dreams you have for your future. Talk about your idea of raising kids, what you think parenting is all about, your idea of spending, if you would want extended family members to spend time at your place regularly or not, hear them out too and decide if that is the way you picture your future to be. Don't disregard or take anything for granted. If you're already in the courting stage, get books on preparing for marriage together, and intentionally talk about everything within boundaries. Yes, everything includes sex too.

10) **Plan and save together**: Money can be a source of serious disagreements even in an already sealed marriage so no, this does not in any way suggest you should open a joint account with your partner. If you are dating to marry, there are a lot of decisions you have to make even before the wedding. Saving money together is one of the productive ways couples feel like they

are in the lives of their partners and feel relevant once there is a mutual agreement on the method adopted. You can agree on a particular amount that you set aside apart from your personal savings, for your future. You and your partner can both have records of the money and the progress you're making. This money can be used for trips together, dates, or specific expenses during your wedding. Everyone should have their own share of the savings kept separately, but hold each other accountable and make sure no one is defaulting. Also plan about your future together, and individually. Help your partner set out goals that will benefit them whether or not you both end up together. Everyone needs the motivation and push to meet deadlines and achieve growth, so seize the opportunity to be your partner's motivation.

11**) Work out together:** Remember how you got very excited the first time you decided to start a workout routine?

Remember how you were so dedicated the first few days till your body started revolting? Well, picture going on your routine with your partner and keeping each other accountable. Having a team member encourages you better to keep up with your fitness plan, and it makes it all the more fun as you would be doing it with someone you love. Pick four days out of seven, set your alarm to ring at the same time, and work out together over a video or voice call. There are apps that help with workout routines and various exercises for women and men respectively. You and your partner would not likely carry out the same exercises, but just do them at the same time and together.

12) **Pray together**: This is important in a relationship especially if you are Christians and want to make God the center of your relationship. Do not disregard the place of prayer in your relationship. There are many issues you cannot solve or handle yourselves and will need the help of God to pull

through them. Praying together gives you the chance to commit your future into the hands of God, pray for your personal life in agreement with another person, and also seek God's counsel and guidance in your relationship. Prayer is a very powerful tool for not just communication with God, but fellowship with another human being. You may not see it immediately, but with time you would realize how much praying with your partner has drawn you both together. You can choose to pray together in the early hours of the morning, set your alarms together, share the same scripture and prayer points and agree on them together. There is hardly any force that can stop such prayers. This is also a good opportunity to share insights on the Scripture, and discuss your religious views. If you are looking forward to a happy and fulfilling marriage, you have to be sure your partner shares the same passion and view about God as you do. This does not mean you will both agree on everything, but make sure their Christianity is not questionable in any way.

CHAPTER FIVE: RULES AND BOUNDARIES

RULES AND BOUNDARIES

It is very true that when the purpose of a thing is not known, abuse is inevitable. Do not make the mistake of not defining your relationship from the onset. It is very easy to neglect this step because of the thrills of romance or the rush of emotions but no matter how hard, it is never too late to take a step back and set rules to guide your relationship.

1) **Define your relationship**: Talk about where the relationship is headed, what you both want or expect, how long you picture it lasting. You'll both also have to talk about what this relationship means to both of you. Is it something just for fun and temporary companionship or are you hoping to go all the way to give this a chance at marriage? No matter how bitter the truth is, it is always best to hear it than live with false hopes only to meet an unavoidable hurt in future. Do not let your desire to be someone special in

the life of your partner make you to just settle for any position. If what they're proposing does not fit what you hoped for, it's better to put an end to the relationship and save yourself from future heartache. Believe me, it would not be worth it.

2) **Talk about sex or like forms of intimacy**: Your partner might be someone who believes he should be able to have sex with his girlfriend, while you on the other hand have always believed that sex should be reserved for marriage only. Do not just jump into your relationship without talking about this first as intimacy is a very serious aspect of a relationship. You can talk to him about the ways you can both be intimate, the extent you can get to, and the lines that should never be crossed till marriage. Your partner has to know your rules when it comes to this point, and you his too. If you both decide to respect each other's boundaries, then you are on for an amazing relationship. Do not start

something blindly only to meet pressure in front. You would also have to state your stand now on sexts or the likes. Do not be scared that you might push them away, or sound too uptight. These are your principles and if anyone feels threatened by them and chooses to leave rather than adjust, then it's best they do. Do not lower your standards for anyone or compromise, else you might regret it in future.

3) **Set the third party rule:** The way you both relate with the opposite sex and things you're both not comfortable with your partner doing, should be discussed too. Do not ignore it as this might become a source of disagreement in future too. The distance between the both of you makes it understandable if you're both going to feel worried that your partner is hanging out with the opposite sex when you don't even have the chance to. Talk about if you are both allowed to hang out with colleagues and friends of the opposite sex, and the limits to what you can do

with them to preserve each other's trust. It is not advised to ask your partner to stay away from his or her friends, be it same gender or not. That would be just too much, so rules guiding their friendship is better. Talk about the things you're both not allowed to discuss with outsiders, how late you can stay out with the opposite sex, or if you would prefer your partner have his hangouts in groups mostly. No matter what you both agree on at this point, trust will play a major role here. You made a decision to be with this person, to love them, build with them, and wait for them. That's literally investing a good period of your life into them. The least you can do is trust them completely as your relationship can hardly stand without solid trust in your partner.

4) **Decide the duration of the long distance:** Inasmuch as your relationship can still thrive no matter the distance, you cannot stay that way forever. Decide with your partner how

long your relationship is meant to be long distance. Is it until your graduation or till after a particular time frame? Which of you will be moving over to the other person to close the gap? Is the other person willing to make the sacrifices necessary if it gets to a point where they have to move? Simple but hard questions like this are necessary to talk about so you know exactly where you're headed in your relationship. Talk about how long you're supposed to date or court before the wedding. Except in rare cases, it is the woman who moves over after the wedding. So talk about it and every other like matter. Are you willing to move, change workplace and leave every life you have in your present location after marriage? It's a pretty tough question but it has to be asked and answered too.

5) **Discuss your likes and major dislikes:** You might think that this extremely charming person can never get on your nerves, but that will not be

the case. For one, your partner is human and is prone to mistakes, so be ready to do lots of forgiving and overlooking. However, there are certain things you will not be caught dead tolerating as a person. Talk about these major dislikes and deal breakers with your partner. State the things you would never condone in your relationship, and listen to them do same. If you love each other, you would make the effort to respect your individual interests and boundaries. It is highly advised to talk about these things so your partner is aware else you cannot have them blamed if eventually they offend you unintentionally.

CHAPTER SIX: SCHEDULING AND SETTING CONSISTENT COMMUNICATION

SCHEDULING AND SETTING CONSISTENT COMMUNICATION

It is truly demanding to be able to keep consistent communication, especially when you and your partner are separated by miles and faced with busy and tight schedules. However, communication is not something you bargain in a relationship. It is highly necessary if not compulsory to keep your communication flowing and your connection alive. Most couple choose specific time to call or video chat every day. This is nice, but if it doesn't work for you, feel free to choose a pattern that works for you. If you're choosing a specific routine for your calls and FaceTime, then be ready to accept that your partner may not be able to always meet up. There are days when unexpected events might come up, emergencies at work, or a particular engagement and you will have to push your talk time further. Understanding and patience is always required of you in any relationship. If you're leaving it to random calls and texts, then fine if that works for you. Just ensure you don't go a day without reaching out to your partner. This communication is all your relationship has to thrive on as physical visits are currently limited. Do not wait for your partner to always reach out to you before you do, and do not make it one person's duty to do so. Shared responsibilities and joint efforts are the key for your relationship to bloom, irrespective of distance. Outside the random calls, share your daily schedule with your partner and decide from then when to have your video calls or long voice calls to share your experiences at the end of every day. Your talk time should involve lots of sharing and lots of listening too. Do not be too engrossed with talking about yourself and your own experiences that you give your partner little or no time to share their own experiences and thoughts. It's one thing to be a very interactive person, it's another thing to be a good listener. Many people lack the ability to listen in a relationship, and they do not realize how this might be hurting their partner and relationship. After a long hard day at work, sometimes all you just want to do is vent and have someone give you their full attention in listening and consoling you. You also have to understand that your partner will want to be pampered. Yes, some days you just literally want to be someone's baby and be treated as such. Words are powerful, and very soothing when the sweetest ones are coming from the one you love.

Another thing you have to know and accept is that your communication with your partner will cost you money to maintain. Airtime, data subscriptions, and SMS charges all boil down to money. Look for easy subscription plans that offer huge bonuses too to enable you minimize your spending and not run into bills because of your relationship. The communication is compulsory, so look for good means to make it happen without hurting your finances. Since you and your partner will be sharing the cost and responsibility for communication, it makes it easier for you to maintain an easy subscription plan. Your communication thriving over a long distance makes it easier to be able to maintain a healthy communication pattern when your partner is finally with you. It can get frustrating when you're always seeing and hearing them but never able to touch them, but the connection you feel from this simple communication is as good as them being physically present with you, so keep it blooming and remember that the distance is just for a period of time.

CHAPTER SEVEN: HOW TO IMPROVE COMMUNICATION

HOW TO IMPROVE COMMUNICATION

Doing the same thing repeatedly over a long period of time can get tiring and uninteresting, especially if you're doing it in the same pattern every day. Which is why you have to be intentional about spicing up your relationship and communication. There are various ways to make your communication with your partner more interesting, creative, and content fun. Feel free to look for spontaneous ideas and act on them. It's your relationship, go ahead and spice it up. This is more interesting when both parties are putting in the efforts together and coming up with great ideas to keep the communication colorful. Some ideas include:

1) **Create new surprises for your partner**: It is really no fun to always be predictable. Seek out new spontaneous ideas to surprise your partner with. Keep them excited and anticipating because they don't know what new surprise you have in store for them. If

you are the last person your partner thinks will ever send a recording of yourself singing, do it. Send personalized cards or electronic ones after customizing. Send them flowers especially if they do not picture you as the kind of person to ever do that. Travel over to see them without notice, if you can afford to. Pick a date when they're extremely stressed or convinced you have so much to do on your part to even have the time to visit. This gesture will be felt deeply by your partner.

2) **Explore varieties**: There are various ways to communicate online with your partner, without having to stick to just phone calls or SMS. If you are yet to get a smart phone, it is advised to get one now and explore the different options you have for communication. Long hours of voice call are nice and very interactive, but you should also explore texting over social media. It helps you keep in touch throughout the day, without having to talk out for others to

hear unless in a case where you're recording a voice note. There is also the option of voice call on various social media platforms, which helps you make calls with your data subscription, rather than your airtime. So if you're looking for how to cut down a bit on airtime used in calling your partner, your next best bet is the voice call option on social media. Then there is the option of video calls which just makes the distance seem lesser as you call. Being able to see your partner regularly and have them see you too is a huge plus and you should explore it to the fullest. Video calls also help you carry out activities together, as you can show your partner the things you're discussing with him about, and have them respond immediately. What's more? Technology just keeps providing extra improvements as there are now various couple apps that help partners in long distance relationships, to feel closer and stay connected. Research on some of these apps, try them out with your partner for fun, and pick the ones that work for you.

3) **Be busy with your own life:** It is very easy to become very clingy especially in this case where your partner is so far away. You might want to fill up every space with the extra talk and tight communication, and this is not healthy. If you keep it up, it would take a toll on you, your partner, and your relationship. It's natural to always want to talk to the one you love, just keep it under watch so you don't go overboard. Get busy with your own life, discover and engage in new activities, get new hobbies, and pursue your own life and career. The tendency to get clingy is higher when you have little or nothing doing in your life which gives you the free time to always be waiting on your partner. If they happen to be very busy and engaged in their own work, you might start to get the feeling that they're acting too busy for you when they're not. So do yourself the good of staying busy too, and pursuing

your personal growth. This does not mean that you should let your career or pursuits affect your relationship and together time with your partner, on the contrary you shouldn't let that happen. Just stay productive in your own life, socialize more with others, keep your life going. Your happiness and progress in your personal life will also determine how your relationship flourishes.

4) **Do not let conflicts linger for too long:** This is something that can easily happen considering the distance between the two of you. Conflicts may become more difficult to solve because all you depend on are online connections and calls to sort out whatever disagreements you have. However, you and your partner will need to practice a high level of understanding for your relationship to work. Try not to let fights drag on for too long. Intentionally set out time to talk about whatever disagreements you've had, if the texts are misinterpreting tones, then try voice

calls or better still video calls which helps you see the reaction of your partner as you speak. In a case where you both feel the need to be physically present to be able to sort out your issues, then take out time off work to visit and sort things out. But it's a big benefit for your relationship if you can sort out disagreements from a long distance, it would make it easier to resolve conflicts in future when you're finally together.

5) **Visit regularly**: No matter how good the communication online is going; regular visits will help your relationship too. It gives you the chance to spend quality time together, to be able to hold and touch your partner, and to make your bond stronger. Visits also make it possible to finally go on physical dates and hangouts together. It also gives you more things to talk about and memories to reminisce over when you're apart, it reassures you and helps your relationship generally.

CHAPTER EIGHT: RELATIONSHIP HACKS

RELATIONSHIP HACKS

Long distance or not, every relationship thrives on certain general rules for relating with another human being. Below are few hacks that will benefit your relationship positively.

1) **Accept your partner:** This is one mistake people make in relationships. They go into a relationship with someone with the mindset of changing them to what they like. It is perfectly okay to support your partners in becoming a better person and working on their flaws, but when you start picking out every imperfection they have and pressuring them to change or become who you selfishly want them to be, it becomes wrong. If you don't love a person for who they are, let them go. Do not tie them down in a relationship and make them feel less of themselves. Accept all the flaws and work with them in improving their lapses. Growing intimacy sometimes starts

with supporting your partner when they are going through a rough patch.

2) **Maintain intimacy:** As simple as hugging or holding of hands may sound, these are strong intimacy builders. Spend time holding hands and taking long walks together, be intentional about tight warm hugs, sit together and talk about everything. Laugh together, play together, hangout together, rest your head on each other's shoulder, keep contact as much as you can. Intimacy is woven into all these simple things that couples mostly overlook.

3) **Carry out activities together:** If you're looking to build your bond more, then engage in various activities together. Go for shows, dates, concerts, football matches (If you're a fan), movie nights, and seminars. Carry out chores together too and share in everything possible together. If you're married, or when you do, make it a thing to bathe with your partner too. Tiny things like

these work miracles in a relationship or marriage.

4) **Never use harsh words on each other:** It's easy to lose control when you're angry or feel hurt. You might think your partner's wrong has earned you the right to talk to them however you like, but that is not right. No matter the conflict or disagreement, discipline yourself to not use harsh words or resolve to name calling. Sort out your issues logically and in a mature manner. Words once said can never be taken back even after you've apologized. Your partner might forgive you, but will have a hard time forgetting that you ever saw them in that light. Also, some people come from homes where quarrels, fights and name calling were regular. Doing anything that might bring back those hurtful memories should be completely avoided as your partner is staying with you to find peace, and not more hurt or crisis.

5) **Compliment and appreciate your partner regularly**: Everyone lives to be appreciated, and it is safe to say words of affirmation is a general love language we all share. Constantly remind your partner of what they mean to you, how much you adore them, how much you are blessed to have them, and how you would pick them all over again if you had the chance. Tell them you love them every day, and never miss the opportunity to compliment them on a new outfit, new hairdo, or any outfit at all when they dress for an occasion. If you're in public, look at them often, touch them, reassure them that your heart is with them and make them know you are proud of them. Take the time to say "Thank you" and show appreciation for whatever they do for you, no matter how tiny. Many people take being appreciated very seriously, so do not try to overlook this or how important it is in your relationship.

CONCLUSION

A relationship of any kind, will need efforts and dedication from both parties to truly thrive and last. It doesn't matter if it's long distance or not, you and your partner will have to be actively involved in building it. What works for one person however, may not work for the other. So take out time to understand yourself, your partner, and figure out what works for your relationship. Crisis will arise, disagreements will come up, just know that all these do not mean an end to your relationship rather they will strengthen your relationship after you have overcome them. It is easier to think you can just keep ending your relationships and moving on to new ones instead of putting effort into resolving issues and making it stronger. Nothing good comes from just wishing and dreaming, so be ready to work out your dream relationship into reality.

The distance might be frustrating and tiring as you set out on this journey. However, if you become intentional about making your relationship beautiful instead of stressing so much about the distance, you will be amazed at how successful and happy your relationship becomes. Use the tools provided for keeping constant communication, show your partner the love and care they deserve even from the distance, be available for them at all times even though you cannot be there physically, and keep them reassured of your love. Trusting in them is crucial for your relationship to last and survive the distance, so do not start poking or doing anything to suggest you mistrust them or give them reasons to mistrust you either. Keep your own social life active, and pursue personal growth. You want to be a better person for your partner and not a liability. So as they pursue their career and grow in their personal lives, do the same for yourself and for them. Make new friends and do not choke up your partner with demands or nagging. It is also important to build a financial dependence for yourself so you do not always fall back on your partner for everything. You would find out how good and confident this makes you feel, and it would make it easier for you to not stay in an abusive relationship just because of fear of where your provision will come from. Whatever you do, remember that this long distance is just for a limited time, and very soon you would be able to spend all the time in the world with your partner.

OTHER BOOKS BY THE SAME AUTHOR

1. 100 Ways to Cultivate Intimacy in Your Marriage: How to Improve Communication, Build Trust and Rekindle Love

2. 200 Ways to Seduce Your Husband: How to Boost Your Marriage Libido and Actually Enjoy Sex: A Couple's Intimacy Guide

3. 232 Questions for Couples: Romantic Relationship Conversation Starters for Connecting, Building Trust, and Emotional Intimacy

4. Communication in Marriage: How to Communicate Effectively With Your Spouse, Build Trust and Rekindle Love

5. 100 Ways to Cultivate Intimacy in Your Marriage: How to Improve Communication, Build Trust and Rekindle Love

6. 40 Bible Verses to Pray Over Your Husband and Marriage: Powerful Scriptural

Prayers for Protection, Guidance, Wisdom, Companionship, Commitment, Healing, and Deliverance

7. Sexual Intimacy in Marriage: 100 Facts Nobody Ever Told You About Sex and Romance [FREE ON KINDLE]

8. How to Build Trust in a Relationship: Powerful Ways to Rebuild Effective Communication, Resolve Conflict, Improve Intimacy, And Avoid Betrayal

9. How to Deal with Husband's Pornography Addiction: Powerful Ways To Help Your Spouse To Overcome & Recover Completely, While Improving Your Sexual Intimacy

10. How to Deal with A Difficult Spouse: Regain Control, Living with a Demanding, Manipulative, and Unappreciative Partner

11. How to Repair a Broken Marriage: Get Back On Your Feet, Bring Back the Lost Passion, And Cultivate a Better Relationship

12. How to Stay Married & Not Kill Your Spouse: Powerful Ways to Deal with Difficult Spouse, Cultivate Happiness in an Unhappy Marriage, & Boost Intimacy

13. How to Get a Divorce & Get Everything: Rules for Successful Separation, Make the Right Decisions, & Build a Perfect Future

14. Couples Money Management Workbook: How to Handle Finances and Save Money for The Future

15. Surviving an Abusive Relationship: How to Deal with Verbal, Emotional & Physical Abuse in A Relationship

Printed in Great Britain
by Amazon